Duroplast in Pastel Colours:
The Trabant

Duroplast in Pastel Colours:

The  Trabant

Jürgen Schiebert   MIXX

Imprint

MIXX - lunch, gifts, entertainment and more
Einsteinufer 63-65 . D-10587 Berlin . tel.: +49-30-34 78 62 40 . fax: +49-30-34 78 62 45
Internet: http://www.mixx.de

Editing, design: D+D Kommunikation Verlag Dirk Nishen GmbH + Co KG
Translated by: Michael Robinson
Printed by: Ruksaldruck, Berlin
Binding: Mathias Wenig, Berlin

ISBN 3-00-002105-1

Contents

Foreword

A great deal was written about him after November 1989: amusing, artistic, ironic - but also superficial and arrogant.

And yet he was a chirpy little chappie, a bit angular and asthmatic, but utterly loveable. He was the number one talking-point for years in the GDR, which was certainly something to do with the fact that you had to wait for him for so long.

And this book is about him - or it - the Trabant, but it is also about the people who constructed and produced the car, in very difficult circumstance but with all the usual Saxon artfulness and skill.

Zwickau has 120,000 inhabitants, and had everything that was needed for the job. It was a textile and coal-mining town until 1904, when August Horch started building cars there, and thus opened a new chapter.

The "Horch men" and the "Audi men", with their decades of experience, were later to provide the necessary core of experience for producing the Trabant. In the days of the GDR the state-owned Sachsenring Automobilwerke in Zwickau became the town's biggest employer. In 1988 every tenth resident worked in the factory.

"Duroplast in pastel colours: the Trabant" will tell you how the Trabant was built, which models were available, the economic and political conditions under which it was built and what work and everyday life were like for the "Sachsenringers", the company's employees.

I was responsible for the firm's public relations from 1981 to the fall of the Berlin Wall in 1989. After 1989 I realized that the Trabant didn't stand a chance on the new, open car market, so I took my chance with Volkswagen.

I dedicate this book to all the Trabant workers, a resourceful and amusing state within the state who tried to work as efficiently as they could. What they achieved under the conditions that I am going to describe deserves unreserved praise.

Jürgen Schiebert

As there was a wait of ten years or more for cars in the GDR, advertising was in fact completely superfluous. But despite this an independent approach to photography developed that was often not without its comic side.

Car building in Zwickau - a long tradition

Perhaps not everybody knows that the GDR's best-known car was built in a town that had a long and successful tradition in the industry. Zwickau in Saxony had been the headquarters of some distinguished companies since the early years of the twentieth century, and so it was possible to use the location and the car-builders' skills under different conditions after the Second World War.

Early days

The development of car-building in Zwickau is inseparably linked with the name of August Horch. With Gottlieb Daimler and Karl Benz - under whom he trained - he was probably the most important pioneer in the German car industry. He was born on 12 October 1868 in the mining community of Winningen, and learned the rudiments of metalwork in the family smithy. His itinerant years took him through southern Germany via Hungary to the Middle East. He entered at the Technikum in Mittweida in 1888, and achieved a high-level pass after six terms. His first contact with car-building was in the Mannheim firm of Benz. Carl Benz promoted him to motor-car manufacturing manager after only four months. This was the start of one of the most significant careers in the German motor industry. Horch soon hit creative barriers with Carl Benz, as Benz was very firmly attached to his own construction principles. And so in October 1899 Horch founded his own company in Cologne, in a stable, interestingly enough. With Hermann Lange, who was to be his partner for many years, he developed his first independent construction techniques and engines here. The first car was ready to drive in late 1900. But by then August Horch had used up all his money, so he moved to Reichenbach in 1902.

This was the year in which the Saxon motor industry was born. He moved to Zwickau early in 1904 and founded A. Horch & Cie., Motorenwagenwerk AG. The conditions were ideal: Zwickau's traditional textile industry invloved a lot of work for little money. Now car-building - a completely new branch of industry - meant hope and an economic upturn.

But August Horch, the great technician, was a bad businessman. Soon voices were raised about the founder of the factory. In the end he was dismissed from his own business on 21 June 1909. The technician had been beaten by the businessmen. But the Horch factory did build some successful cars in these turbulent years. Dr. Rudolf Stöss won the Herkomer run - a fore-runner of today's rallies - in a Phaeton 18/22 hp, in 1906. Only normal touring cars were allowed to take part. Three criteria were evaluated: comfort and appearance, speed, and hill-climbing. Even in those days extreme conditions led to new developments that could exploited in production vehicles, just as they are today.

At that time horses were the car-drivers' great enemy. August Horch remembered in his memoirs: "In the early days of the car it was sim-

ply not possible to drive past horses, even at walking-pace, every animal shied for a moment, and older people who were involved will remember the remarkable phenomenon that when they shied the animals jumped at cars as though they were going to attack them." But despite bitter clashes, some involving hand-to-hand fighting, between coachmen and drivers, the triumphant march of the car could not be halted for any longer.

After being stripped of power in his own factory, Horch opened "August Horch Autombilwerke GmbH Zwickau" on 16 July 1909, although shortly afterwards he lost a case brought against him by his first company because the names were the same. So Horch latinized the imperative of the German verb horchen (horch! - audi!) and thus found himself a name for the new firm. Thus "Audi Automobilwerke GmbH" became the second motor-car business in Zwickau. Audi built its first four-cylinder vehicle in 1910. The C-Type had almost no competition on the Austrian Alpine Run, and went into automobile history as the "Alpine Victor". In subsequent years both Zwickau businesses made a significant contribution to the structural and technical

Factory drivers assembling outside the offices at the Horch factory in Zwickau after the 1921 Avus race. Horch cars were taking part in so-called reliability trials as early as 1904.

development of the motor-car. At the same time an outstanding team of specialist workers emerged whose achievements brought world-wide fame to the names of Horch and Audi.

The twenties

Horch devoted more and more time to organization during the First World War, and was a member of several committees dealing with automotive matters. His last major technical achievement was shifting the steering-wheel from the right- to the left-hand side of the car.

View of the Horch machine shop in 1925. The traditional system using drive machine (transmission belts on the ceiling) - working machine was to give way to a new generation of machine tools shortly after this; the new system tripled the output speed of the workshop.

Both the Horch and the Audi factories urgently needed to re-organize production and to introduce methods and procedures that were competitive but also ensured that their products developed technically. Henry Ford had introduced the conveyor-belt in the USA, which cleared the way for mass production. The transition from the workshop to the conveyor-belt principle meant shorter production and transport times, reduced the amount of work and also the space required. In addition to this plant was modernized and parts were classified by type and standardized. The Americans were largely in the forefront of this know-how. It meant above all that they could produce cars at reasonable prices, even if they could not match the high quality of the best German models. The German car industry - especially in Saxony - was increasingly faced with financial difficulties. Technical innovations, like the first German eight-cylinder production car, built by Paul Daimler at Horch, or Audi's Pullmann-Limousines, did solve the money problems.

In 1929 a Dane called Jörgen Skafte-Rasmussen acquired a majority shareholding in Audi. He had already been very successful with the DKW motor bikes, and now he was trying to transfer the strategy he had used there to the car industry. A small car with front-wheel drive was created, using the DKW two-stroke engine. The first prototype was ready after a development period of just six months. This car, christened the "DKW F1", was launched at the Berlin Motor Show in February 1931. A total of 250,000 of the DKW F1 to F8 models were built from 1931 to 1942; the construction principles and engine of the last of these can be considered the ancestor of the Trabant.

Auto-Union

The world economic crisis exacerbated the German car industry's problems. Cars were a luxury in Germany again; only a very few people could afford them, and this meant that the bottom fell out of sales. Thus the car firms in Saxony were compelled to think about working together. The Auto Union was one of Germany's biggest automobile concerns, and came into being in Chemnitz on 29 July 1932. But the individual firm names and their production profile were retained under the four-ring trade mark. Horch produced high-performance, prestigious eight-cylinder cars, Audi became the main producer of elegant front-wheel drive cars, Wanderer made a name for itself with reliable middle-range vehicles and DKW produced motor bikes and also small cars in the lowest price bracket that distinguished themselves by progressive engineering and low fuel consumption. The business had been transformed into a Saxon state concern with 75% bank participation; it co-

The Horch factory's first series production eight cylinder vehicle, built by Paul Daimler, caused a sensation in 1926. The 303 model was followed by 39 variants, which were attractive because of their reasonable price as well as their exemplary technology. This is a 1930 limousine, in a 70s publicity photograph.

ordinated the production programme for the individual makes from motor bike to luxury cars, the latter remaining the province of the Horch factory in Zwickau.

The eight-cylinder cars produced by Horch were leaders in their class. The milestone was the first 830 model V8 in 1933, then the 830 BL, of which 6,124 were produced from 1935 to 1940. The 853 sports convertible, created by sculptor Wilhelm Böhm and designer Günter Mickwausch, was particularly highly esteemed. But the Horch range also included some supercharged engines. Horch produced a 12 cylinder car (models 600 and 670) to compete with the big Mercedes and Maybach vehicles. About 80 of these cars, each 5.4 metres long and weighing 2.3 tons, were produced from 1931 to 1934. They developed 120 horsepower with a cubic capacity of 6.021. Top speed was 140 kph, at which 26 litres of fuel passed through the carburettor.

Audi's particular field was front-wheel drive cars, which DKW worked up for series production in Germany. The Audi 225 model with front-wheel drive had a six-cylinder four-stroke engine in 1935 with a cubic capacity of 2.255; it developed 55 hp, and its top speed was 100 kph.

DKW produced Europe's cheapest car - it cost 1,685 reichsmarks. As well as front-wheel drive the DKWs had a "Dynastart" (motor-generator) system which was starter and dynamo in one, and was used in Zwickau up to the P70, which was discontinued in 1958. Demand exceeded production for the first time in 1937. Delivery times of three to four months had to be accepted for DKWs. At the time it would have been impossible even to dream that they would extend to 10 to 12 years for the Trabant.

DKW convertible with "mother-in-law seat".

But Auto Union achieved its real fame with spectacular record-breaking feats and Grand Prix successes. The duels between Daimler-Benz and Auto Union were legendary. Ironically enough Dr. Ferdinand Porsche's Stuttgart office took over Auto Union's development work. The V-16 engines developed 295 hp at first, which was later increased to 520 hp. The employees in the Horch racing department in Zwickau in particular came in for a great deal of praise, as well as the design engineer. They built the racing car, which was made up of 1,622 parts, in a mere eight months. Hans Stuck broke three records even on his first outing in March 1934. From 1934 to 1939 Auto Union acquired 18 Grand Prix records. There were also numerous victories in circuit and mountain racing. In 1937 Auto Union held all the records in the 3,000 to 8,000 cc classes. Ultra-modern technology and excellent streamlining enabled the Auto Union fireballs to compete against Mercedes' performance advantages. Their drivers included excellent performers like Ernst von Delius, H.P. Müller, Rudolf Hasse, Achille Varzi and Tazio Nuvolari, as well as Stuck and Bernd Rosemeyer. The outbreak of the Second World War signalled the end of the great international motor-racing events.

The start of armaments production saw the beginning of an inglorious period for Auto Union. Horch built jeeps and personnel carriers and light armoured scout cars. From 1943 to 1945 they produced nothing but armoured personnel carriers with half-track chassis, a total of 7,131 vehicles. The Audi factory made the 1.500 A lorry for the army. Numerous foreign workers and inmates of the Flossenbürg concentration camp were forced to work in the factory, sometimes under humiliating and inhumane conditions. In late 1944 Horch employed 10,330 men and women and Audi 2,600. The Zwickau factories were bombed in Anglo-American air-raids in October and November 1944, which reduced half the production capacity to rubble.

Production increased considerably in the 30s. This photograph was taken on 12 October 1939 and shows DKWs parked in the open air at the Audi factory.

A difficult new start

The "popular referendum on the appropriation without compensation of businesses belonging to war criminals and Nazi activists" was held on 30 June 1946. The SED had been founded shortly before and achieved its manipulated goal: 77.6% of the electorate voted for appropriation.

Zwickau was first occupied by the Americans at the end of the war in 1945, but they shortly handed command to the Soviets. As Auto Union had produced a not inconsiderable quantity of military vehicles and armaments, the company was subject to reparation laws. A large number of valuable machines and documents were confiscated and taken to the Soviet Union. This largely removed the basis for material production. After "compensation" work, which lasted until mid-March 1946, attention was turned to creating new jobs. And so a repair shop was set up in the ruins of each of the two factories, mainly to refurbish Red Army and Soviet service vehicles. Workers recovered materials and tools from the ruins. These commissions meant that the highly qualified teams of specialist workers could be kept together. They kept their heads above water by producing agricultural and domestic equipment like harrows, cow chains, sack carts, stoves and coarse grain mills.

Repairing vehicles for the Soviet Military Administration (SMAD) formed the basis for the reconstruction of the completely shattered transport business. The Horch and Audi factories were ordered to produce spare parts

as well as carrying out repairs.

SMAD's No. 2 Order of 10 June 1945 authorized anti-Fascist and democratic parties and trade unions in the Soviet occupation zone and Berlin. This authorization was of course not democratic as such. Merging the SPD (German Socialist Party) and the KPD (German Communist Party) to form the SED (German Socialist Unity Party - the East German Communist Party) in particular was forced through and passed at the Party

Unification Conference on 21 and 22 April 1946. Appropriation of former arms firms without compensation was also built into this campaign. A so-called popular referendum on this was held in Saxony on 30 June 1946. 77.6 of those entitled to vote voted "Yes". This referendum formed the basis for the nationalization of "businesses belonging to Nazis and war criminals". The Auto Union works also passed into the "hands of the people" at this time. A little later August Horch had to fight against accusations by the SED. Unproven assertions presented him as a "Nazi activist and war criminal". Massive pressure resulted in the withdrawal of his status as a freeman of the city of Zwickau.

Vehicle production slowly got under way again. The first vehicle to be produced in the Horch factory was the H3 lorry. It was made of left-over materials, and could carry a maximum of 3 tons. The 4.2 litre four-stroke Otto engine had six cylinders and developed 100 hp. The factory workers built 853

So-called "visible agitation" by the SED outside the Horch factory in Zwickau, now appropriated and nationalized. Party propaganda attempting to brand August Horch as a war criminal had not failed to take its effect.

The H3 lorry was the first type of vehicle to be produced in Zwickau after the war. It was made of pre-war materials.

lorries of this type from 1947 to 1949. In 1948 the Industrial Vehicle Construction Department (Industrieverwaltung Fahrzeugbau; IFA - (later GDR Industrial Vehicle Construction Department) was established. Thus East German automobile manufacture was centralized.

Another achievement - more in terms of propaganda than production - originated in Saxony and was still effective in the 60s. Face-worker Adolf Hennecke in the Oelnitz coal mine exceeded his work-norm by 380 percent on 13 October 1948, which was greeted with jubilation by the party.

The "Hennecke method", triggered by Oelsnitz miner Adolf Hennecke, was also introduced into the automobile industry. Thorough preparation and getting ready tools - which were by no means always available - and the appropriate material meant that "young activists" could exceed the existing norms. And their reward was not just applause . . .

This voluntary and masterly performance was intended to spur all firms on to produce more. The SED commented as follows: "The Hennecke movement is a new form of the class struggle. It makes the work-place into a barricade and the activist, carrying the banner of the new age, into a hero of every day and of labour." Originally a miner called Sepp Wenig had been intended to work this precisely prepared shift. But how would the "Wenig (wenig = little, not much) movement" or "Wenig method" have sounded?

Horch and Audi workers accepted the Hennecke method - though this was often forced upon them. So-called thrust actions reduced working time and increased production in the "Hennecke shifts".

On 17 February 1949 the SED decided to improve the output of the Machine-Rental-Station (Maschinen-Ausleih-Stationen; MAS) in agriculture (later called MTS - Machine-Tractor-Station). Compulsory collectivization, the so-called "democratic land reform", had produced enormous fields. But there were no machines to cultivate them. MAS's basic equipment consisted of hundreds of lorries and 1,000 tractors from the Soviet Union. The 1,001st tractor had to come from the Soviet occupation zone whatever happened. The Horch factory was commissioned to build a 40 hp tractor at short notice. This was resisted by a lot of workers as they saw themselves as car-builders, not blacksmiths. This jolted the SED into an agit-prop action. Numerous firms were committed to help under slogans like "Help for Horch is work for peace" and "The Zone needs Horch - Horch needs the Zone". The trade union

built up a group of "tractor activists" in the factory itself. The first tractor was handed over on 21 May 1949 and was given the highly allusive name "Pioneer". The four-cylinder four-stroke diesel engine with petrol starter developed 40 hp at 1,250 rpm. 2,605 were produced by January 1951, when production was shifted to Nordhausen.

The first tractor produced in Zwickau was handed over on 21 May 1949. It was called the "Pioneer".

The situation in the field of commercial vehicles was also complicated in the Soviet Occupation Zone. Only producers of light lorries like Framo and Phänomen had their factories in East Germany. This made it necessary to develop their own lorry industry. Thus, after production of the H3 the Horch factory was tooled up for lorry production. The H3 A went into series production in October 1950. It had a four-stroke diesel engine developing 80 hp. The rate at which production increased is interesting: in 1950 only 150 lorries came off the conveyor belts, in 1951 it was already up to 2,000. By 1958 31,361 H3 A models had been produced. It is remarkable in

The S 4000.

this context that even in 1955 81 per cent of lorries in the GDR were over 15 years old.

The S 4000, the model developed from the H3 A, went into series production in 1958. The maximum load was raised to 4 tons and the payload area by 10 per cent. 2,075 lorries of this type were produced in 1958/59. Production of commercial vehicles in Zwickau was discontinued after the S4000-1 lorry. This had a 5-speed synchromesh gearbox and developed 90 hp. 3,192 of these vehicles had been produced by 1959. A nationalized company called "Ernst Grube" in nearby Werdau took over production in the same year. The S4000-1 later became a cab-over-engine lorry developed in Ludwigsfelde near Berlin as the W 50. The Zwickau works built series EM 4 diesel engines in the fifties as well as lorries, and also petrol engines. If one remembers that the IFA F 9

The IFA F 8 was the first private car produced in Zwickau after the war. It was identical with the pre-war DKW F 8 model. The F8 was a popular and much driven vintage car in GDR in the 70s and 80s, with owners often organized in regional clubs.

motor-car model later formed the basis for the "Wartburg", it is clear that the cradle for all motor vehicle production in the GDR was Zwickau, with very few exceptions.

Of course the Zwickau automobile industry was mainly concerned with producing private cars. The IFA F8 was the first vehicle in this field after the war. It corresponded with the DKW F8, which had been produced before the war. The F8 had a two-cylinder, two-stroke, water-cooled engine, front-wheel drive, 69 cc cubic capacity, three forward gears and a reverse gear. It

developed 20 hp, and the wooden bodywork had some artificial leather covering. It was produced in limousine, convertible, luxury convertible and estate versions. The convertible was also obtainable with sheet steel bodywork. The Audi factory produced 26,254 of these models from 1949 to 1955. The successor model, the F9, was the first joint production by Horch and Audi. Horch built the bodywork and Audi assembled the vehicle. It had a three-cylinder three-stroke engine that developed 28 hp with a cubic capacity of 900 cc. This was enough for speeds of 110 kph. From 1949 to 1953 1,625 vehicles were built, then production was shifted to Eisenach. There the F9 formed the basis for the equally popular "Wartburg".

Private car manufacture in Zwickau peaked again with the P 240. Various "comfort elements" could be enjoyed in this top-of-the-range motor car: reclining seats, separate heating for driver and passengers, continuously variable instrument illumination, anti-dazzle internal rear-view mirror with reading lamp. The P 240 had a water-cooled six-cylinder Otto engine developing 80 hp from a cubic capacity of 2,407 cc. This meant that the car, which had a four-speed synchromesh gearbox, could effortlessly reach 140 kph. The vehicle had torsion bar suspension and weighed 1,480 kg. It became known

The P 240 was the only genuine development of the luxurious pre-war Horch models, but only 1,382 examples of this model were produced between 1954 to 1959, used primarily by party and state functionaries.

In 1955, 15 employees of the factory climbed on to the P 70 to demonstrate the resilience of the material known as "Duroplast". At first this plastic material was made of wood pulp, cotton waste and PVC, and later of a mixture of phenolic resin and low-grade cotton.

as the "Sachsenring", and was used mainly as a vehicle for functionaries and for prestige purposes. Only 1,382 had been produced by 1959.

Development work on a plastic to replace imported steel body sheets had been under way since 1951. Kurt Lang, who was the managing director of IFA at the time, appointed a research group, which included Wofgang Barthel, Fritz Hans and Erich Klaus, as well as Lang himself. After six months a compression moulding material consisting of wood pulp, cotton waste and PVC had been "mixed". Later the thermoplastic material was replaced by a Duroplast (pressure setting plastic) material based on phenolic resin, reinforced with cotton.

The first car with Duroplast bodywork was the P 70, which was introduced in 1955. The carcass was made of wood and covered with plastic, which was screwed on to the timber frame. The P 70 was developed from the IFA F8, but was at the same time the first independent post-war development in the private car field. Its technical specifications were entirely in tune with the standards of the times, and the bodywork caused quite a stir. 36,063 vehicles were built from 1955 to 1959, in the form of limousines, estate cars or coupés.

I had a P 70 coupé in the mid 80s. I bought it for 3,000 marks, and it was a trusty companion. Although it was already 30 years old it had been well looked after and was in its original condition. It wasn't even particularly difficult to get spares. I placed a few ads and got almost everything from former F8 and P70 owners - from a complete engine to the original bulbs. One very sensitive part was the gear change box with three forward and one reverse gears, which was blocked on to the motor. It was also known as the "Christmas tree" because of its shape. Changing gear called for a certain empathy and required double de-clutching. Fortunately there will still a few workshops in the GDR that repaired F8s and P70s, and who had the necessary contacts to have new gearboxes made as well as the appropriate specialized tools.

A procedure that always attracted a few curious people was topping up the gearbox lubricant. You either bought "10 GF" prepared in tins, or mixed 2/3 ambroleum and 1/3 motor oil yourself. The filler hole was on the gearshift dome. I used to put in the jelly-like lubricant with a dessert spoon, which regularly produced the question: "Are you feeding your car?" It was advisable not to use the P 70 too often in winter. The salt that was always spread on the roads in the GDR corroded the floor and above all the

The author's P 70 coupé.

exposed brake cable, and the heater could only clear the windscreen and windows to a certain extent. This was no different with the Trabant, as the heater was fed from the exhaust or the front silencers. But I had some wonderful drives in the summer - even from Zwickau to the Baltic. The P70, and the coupé in particular, were rarely seen on the road in 1985, and every second person who overtook me gave me a thumbs-up sign through the window.

The seat covering and interior trim was leather, and the side windows could be fully lowered. The fuel tank, which was in the engine compartment, held 32 litres. Driven appropriately a full tank of the 1:25 mixture would take you 400 km. While the coupé had a genuine boot, you could only get to the equivalent in the "Zwickau" limousine by folding the rear of the back seat down, in other words from the interior. Loading bulky items was by no means simple. The IFA F8 had a V6 engine, but the P70's was a V12. The motor-generator, which worked as a starter and as a dynamo, was reliable. The engine started a few seconds after pressing the starter button, with a typical clattering two-stroke noise. The P 70 also had a manually operated free-wheel device.

Changing gear, as I have mentioned above, required a certain amount of skill. The following instructions appeared in the manual:

Changing into 2nd gear -

> *When the car has reached a speed of 15 kph in 1st gear, take*
>
> *your foot off the accelerator pedal and disengage the clutch at*
>
> *the same time. Move the gear-shift into neutral, wait briefly*
>
> *until the revs have decreased a little, shift into 2nd gear, slowly*
>
> *re-engage the clutch and accelerate briskly at the same time.*
>
> **Note:** *Be very careful when shifting out of 1st gear not to*
>
> *engage reverse. This would destroy the gearbox. Care should*
>
> *therefore be taken that when shifting from 1st to 2nd gear the*
>
> *gear-shift is only moved into the neutral position, then drawn*
>
> *backwards and only then moved to the right to engage 2nd*
>
> *gear."*

Once you had grasped this the car was great fun to drive, even 30 years later. And 90 kph wasn't all that slow on GDR motorways.

The "Trabant" became world famous as a "plastic bomber" in later years. Only a few people know that the P 70 was the first of its kind. Here too the instruction manual provide some very illuminating information:

"The VEB (Volkseigener Betrieb: Publicly Owned Concern) Sachsenring Automobilwerke Zwickau has broken new ground with the P 70 model. The body frame is made of wood, and Duroplast has been used for the body for the first time in series production. These achievements are hailed a pioneering work by engineers, researchers and workers in the German Democratic Republic throughout the car-building world. The new material has important advantages over sheet metal, including:

- *low weight*
- *good heat insulation*
- *good vibration or silencing properties*
- *absolute weather resistance and*
- *an extraordinary degree of elasticity.*

. . . The P 70 is classed as a small car in terms of its horse-power, but the size of its passenger accommodation brings it close to the border with medium-sized vehicles. Even long journeys in the P 70 are pleasant and relaxing."

The Trabant takes its bow . . .

Small cars as such were nothing new. They were quick to experience an unexpected boom world-wide. Wanderer built a private car as early as 1911 with two seats arranged one behind the other. In 1922 another two-seater came on to the market in the form of the Citroen 5 CV, followed by Hanomag's "Kommißbrot" ("Army Loaf") in 1925. Small cars enjoyed their heyday in Germany with the DKW in the thirties. The Fiat 500 "Topolino" was no less successful. When the "economic miracle" brought new prosperity in the mid 50s, the demand for individual motorized transport became more vociferous. So there was a short period with a positive flood of bubble cars in West Germany. Messerschmidt, Heinkel, BMW, NSU, Sachs and the Hans Glas KG (Goggomobil) were the best-known manufacturers.

The political basis

A different approach was taken in East Germany. A plan for "Economics in the Motor Car Industry" was developed by the Ministry of General Machine Construction, based on critical analysis of the starting situation, and thus accessible only to a few functionaries; it identified problems and made suggestions for solutions. This work was of course based on the "Socialist Economics" developed by Marx and Engels and refined to a certain extent by Lenin. It was built around a command economy and started on a false theoretical basis. This can be proved simply by the fact that an economy of short supply - with the exception of party and propaganda literature - was inherent in it.

In their introduction to "Economics in the Motor Car Industry" the authors, under the chairmanship of Kurt Lang, the former managing director of IFA, stated: "Setting up a strong publicly-owned industry under the difficult conditions of the post-war period was an extraordinarily significant achievement. It could only be brought about by the power of the workers and farmers in creative co-operation between the working class and the intelligentsia. The result of this work of reconstruction was that gross industrial production in the German Democratic Republic was successfully and significantly increased in 1954 vis-à-vis the pre-war situation. ... Thus at the time of writing a further upturn in publicly-owned industry is essentially dependent on how successful we are in overcoming inadequacies that still exist in the organization and management of the individual branches of industry. The principal cause of these inadequacies lies in the fact that insufficient attention has been paid to the requirements of objective economic laws under the conditions of the period of transition from capitalism to socialism. In order to find organizational forms and management methods appropriate to the industry's present state of development it is no longer sufficient to examine the general phenomena of economic laws, to study the effect of economic laws in the different branches of industry and to develop specific organizational forms and management methods for the particular branches of industry from this."

What was being expressed here in a roundabout way was a fundamental flaw in socialist economics: it was not always the experts who had their say, but often inadequate comrades. This does not mean that all SED members were inadequate, on the contrary, the level of education in the party was quite high. But precisely in the field of "organization and management" a certain dilettante quality, which reached its peak in Günter Mittag, could not be mistaken. The people involved, who were aware of the real reasons for faulty business practices, were not allowed to mention them, because different economic developments could only have been brought about by changing the system entirely.

The GDR's first small car: the Youth Organization of the VEB Automobilwerke Zwickau handed over a P 70 as a gift on the occasion of the "VIth World Youth Games" in Moscow in 1956.

The study quoted above identified crucial weaknesses. For example, supply of materials to the firms was not planned, and so there were corresponding slack periods caused by delivery delays. Time delays, flaws in quality and fundamentally antiquated production techniques were also cited by the authors. A well as this, the "workers" were inadequately motivated to take an active part in designing and improving production processes. But as well as organizational and management problems there were considerable disproportions in production itself, as automated plant and manual manufacturing

One of the first "plastic bombers" from Zwickau. The first P 70 series went into production in 1957, when it was christened "Trabant" ("Satellite").

phases were placed side by side - with the result that, for example, 55,000 private cars could be put together annually in the assembly shop, while on 10,000 units were built in the engine, chassis and bodywork shops.

Even when a whole series of faults were identified - no one ever questioned "the economic fundamentals of socialism". But when one recalls that the insights quoted at the beginning of this chapter were put on to paper in 1955, then it is clear that the authors had almost prophetic powers. They were listing fundamental deficits of socialist production methods. But it was also essential in a paper like this to get in a good dig at capitalism as well.

It is a marginal gloss in economic history to point out that more cars are now produced per year in Germany by "anarchic capitalist production methods" than were produced throughout the 40 years of the GDR.

It is astonishing how openly the "Economics" paper demanded a management attitude that, although it was couched in actual "socialist" language actually hit the nail on the head in places: "The statement by the first deputy of the Minister of Motor car, Tractor and Agricultural Machinery Construction is entirely valid for the correct training of the cadres; he declared extraordinarily emphatically: ‚We must train the directors of the individual departments of the ministry in such a way that they never become prisoners of their own apparatus. . . . All Ministry employees must be aware who is the manager, that the manager does not allow himself to be pushed around, that he takes the initiative himself and is in a position to make a correct decision and does not support everything that other people want. It is essential that a manager does not do all the work himself, but directs his energies to stimulating and furthering his fellow-workers' initiatives."

Thus the authors were aware of social, economic and organizational faults. But who was going to present these truths to those actually empowered to make decisions - the Polit-bureaucrats? At a time when there had to be jubilation at least to draw a veil over inadequacies, where agitation and propaganda were well ahead of reality and had long since established themselves as independent entities?

The P 50 and P 60

A car of one's own, as a means of individual mobility, played an important part as a status symbol in the GDR as well. Private car development and production in the GDR started with the P 70. It was to be followed by further, newly developed models. Of course this process had to start by analysing national and international car production, in order to establish premises for building a competitive small car. Comparisons with other makes of car and the requirements derived from them were to be seen as an absolutely positive aspect of a command economy. This was the actual theoretical basis for private car development. So far, so good. In subsequent years the problem was that these requirements could not be implemented either technically or in terms of construction. The economy was too weak for this, and there were not enough people and above all no one was brave enough to convey to the "powers-that-be" that the command economy was gradually leading to paralysis. And any one who was brave enough was very quickly removed from any position of responsibility.

The P 50 in the loading-bay.

Back to where we started. Private cars and small cars in particular were defined as followed in the paper on "Economics":

"Private cars -

> *Private cars are predominantly intended for the use of the workers. The GDR has the task in the field of private cars of considerably raising production and at the same time drastically increasing technical specifications and quality while simultaneously reducing costs. This is a very important economic task. In order to form a clear picture of the various classes of private car it is appropriate to survey the product across its whole range.*

Small cars -

> *Small cars are the lowest class of private car. In this case it is essential to pay attention to the thesis of "limitation to what is possible in a private car". When deciding upon the technical conception and fittings for a small car it is therefore necessary always to work towards a motor vehicle that is as cheap as possible. Nevertheless the small car should not represent a primitive solution, but must be a fully valid means of transport with adequate driving qualities and an appropriate degree of comfort when travelling. Thus its development makes the acutest possible demands on construction and production.*
>
> *The following technical specifications for small cars emerge from existing modern models:*
> * *on-the-road weight   -   600 kg max.*
> * *two-stroke engine   -   400-500 cc*
> * *performance   -   14-20 hp*
> * *power-weight ratio   -   35-30 kg/hp*
>
> *Lightweight construction and group building methods are needed to achieve this, i.e.:*
>
> * *front- or rear-wheel drive*
> * *two-cylinder, two-stroke engine, air-cooled*
> * *the best and simplest suspension
>   (prospectively rubber or combination suspension)*
> * *plastic bodywork"*

The required top speed for the new vehicle was 85 kph. In the mid 50s this was very much what was generally expected.

The design engineers used the insights they had acquired when they started to develop a new and efficient small car in the mid 50s, under the direction of Walter Haustein and Wilhelm Orth. All this of course happened under the beady eye of the party, which influenced the engineers' work in countless conversations and arguments. Thus a long life-span, high utility value and simple maintenance and servicing were named as important factors. But the party also introduced one demand into the catalogue of requirements that effectively ruled out the development of new models: the small car was to be based on a structure that was open to development without expensive change. And this policy of the "1000 small steps" domi-

nated the Trabant until production ceased. It remained the same car throughout its 34-year history.

In West Germany bubble cars boomed in the 50s, as they could be produced at reasonable prices and in large numbers. But in East Germany car manufacturers wanted to produce a four-seater small car from the outset, with low-wearing construction that was easy to service. However, it was necessary to rely on the production possibilities offered by existing, antiquated plants.

Of course political and ideological preparations had to be made for the production of the "New One". So a group of P 50 youth activists was formed and a competition announced for the 40th anniversary of the "Great Socialist October Revolution" - the day on which the first P 50 was to come off the production line.

Demonstration of the "Duroplast" cladding.

Employees were invited to find a suitable name for the new car. Some curious suggestions were submitted, like "Muldeperle" (the name of a river in Zwickau), "Zwickel" (actually spandrel, gusset, but reminiscent of Zwickau), "Lux", or even "Robert-Schumann-Car", as Schumann was born in Zwickau. But finally the panel chose the name "Trabant" ("Satellite"), suggested by the launch of the first artificial satellite, which went into history as "Sputnik", by the Soviet Union.

The first Trabant came off the production line as planned on 7 November 1957. 50 cars had been produced by the end of the year. The new car also required changes in technique and technology. For example, a turning device was built into the final stage of the assembly line. This meant that the fitters no longer had to carry out physically difficult work on the underside of the car above their heads, which lead to a rise in quality and reduced accident potential. The technical requirements for large-scale production of the Trabant were gradually met. Here extension of the plant area had a considerable part to play. A shop with an area of 10,000 square metres was built, at an investment level of over 3 million marks. The number of employees increased as well. In 1951 Audi/AWZ employed 1,250 car-builders, by 1957 there were already 2,500. At Horch/VEB Sachsenring the figures rose from 4,000 to 5,250 in the same period.

The Trabant P 50

The material looking like rolled-up carpets on the left of the photograph is the mixture of cotton and resin that was loaded into the "waffle-irons" that can be seen in the background. The body parts that the worker is loading on to this cart were then produced under heat and pressure.

The P 50 introduced a new, and, if you wish, the final phase of car building in Zwickau - it was to last just under 34 years. The P 50 was a logical development of the DKW series, especially as far as the engine was concerned. It was air-cooled, rather than water-cooled. An axial fan driven by a V-belt from the camshaft blew cooling air round the cylinders. It was a very simple, but reliable principle: if water-cooling was used the radiator could freeze or overheat, so more water was needed. The Trabant was independent of this. A particularly striking feature was the new car's Duroplast bodywork. Duroplast was a mixture of phenolic resin and cotton, which was "baked" to form a stable mass. The Duroplast parts used to cover the basic frame were made in pieces of equipment that really did look like oversize waffle-irons.

Trabant P 50 - technical data

Engine	-	*two-cylinder two-stroke Otto engine*
Bore	-	*66 mm*
Stroke	-	*73 mm*
Cubic capacity	-	*500 cc*
Compression	-	*6.7*
Power	-	*18 hp at 3750 rpm*
Camshaft	-	*arranged in threes in roller bearings*
Big-end bearing	-	*roller bearing*
Mixture	-	*petrol: oil = 25:1*
Cooling	-	*air-cooled*
Gearbox	-	*gear change box*
Gearshift	-	*floor-mounted*
Braking	-	*interior block drum brakes*
Overall length	-	*3375 mm*
Overall width	-	*1500 mm*
Overall height	-	*1395 mm*
Unladen weight	-	*620 kg*
Payload	-	*330 kg*
Max. speed	-	*90 kph*
Consumption	-	*6-7l/100 km*

Production had to be restructured in order to increase Trabant output as much as possible. One requirement was to shift previous production elsewhere or to discontinue existing ranges. For this reason the Automobile Construction Department at the Ministry for General Machine Construction suggested that the two Zwickau factories should be combined. The advantages were "expedient organization of production, better use of existing plant and simplification and cost reduction in administration and transport and better use of the workforce."

One of the first advertising photographs ever taken of the P 50. There was always a bit of nature in the picture, and an attractive woman was obligatory.

It is interesting to see how this move, which was seen by many old "Horchers" and "Audianers" as an enforced merger, was dressed up politically. This is how "Automobilbauer einst und jetzt" (Car-builders then and now), a work that toed the party line, summed up the mood about the coming unification: "Not all workers were immediately enthusiastic about this. Great ideological support came from comrades at regional and district level at the time. Discussions with party leaders from the two factories and comrades and colleagues from production took place ten days apart. The party took issue with ideas that originated in the capitalist past. Thus for example the proposition that VEB Sachsenring would "gobble up" the Automobilwerke - the large eating the small. The motto cultivated by the Imperialists: "Audi here - Horch there" was still floating around a few heads. The party leadership constantly emphasized the fundamental difference between the despotic regime of exploitation practised by the concerns and motor car construction under socialist conditions in the workers' and peasants' state." . . .

But if production was to be increased substantially it really was essential to merge the two firms. This significant step took place on 1 May 1958: VEB Sachsenring, formerly Horch, and VEB Automobilwerke Zwickau (AWZ), formerly Audi, became the VEB Sachsenring Automobilwerke Zwickau. Herbert Uhlmann became factory director, and was succeeded after

his death in 1974 by Günter Hipp. Winfried Sonntag was technical director, Adolf Hempel labour director. Rudolf Grundmann was production manager, Richard Wetzel the chief accountant and Manfred Hanke the planning director.

Work in the new, large factory was based on pronouncements by the Vth SED party conference, which took place in July 1958 and fixed various matters including economic policy for the next five years. The euphoric demand was made at this conference that socialism in the GDR should be swept to its final victory and the "period of transition from capitalism to socialism" should be concluded. "Socialist production conditions" were to be implemented throughout the economy. More and more slogans were to

The 1958 product range, from the left: Trabant P 50, P 70, estate version, P 70 limousine with fabric roof, P 240 "Sachsenring", H3 A. S 4000-1.

Sport and games equipment was also made by the VEB until well into the 60s. This photograph shows ice-skate manufacture.

motivate the workforce to believe in the socialist future. An appropriate comment was made by the Soviet writer Fadejew: "Social Realism - God knows what that is."

The Trabant was with the citizens of the GDR throughout the socialist period until November 1989. It was every family's dearest wish to have one, even though they were technically out of date after a few years. In 1959 it cost 7,450 marks. In international terms that was a reasonable price, in the GDR it was a white-collar worker's annual income. For its time the P 50 was a car that could hold its own in international comparisons. It was acceptably roomy, and its parameters were appropriate to the standards of its class. 130,000 P 50s came off the production line between 1958 and October 1962. By 1961 almost 3,000 Trabants had been exported to the West, to countries including Holland, Belgium, Denmark and West Germany.

Painting a P 50 body in 1960.

Handing over a Trabant P 50 in 1959 t the GDR's most popular sportsman, racing cyclist Täve Schur.

A popular anecdote shows the considerable difference there was at the time between the plastic bomber from Zwickau and an American limo: an American orders a Trabant in Zwickau. Four months later it arrives in New York. The American smiles quietly to himself: "Those East Germans! They even send you a model in advance."

The first variant on the P 50, the Trabant P 50/1, had new front seats, the wipers covered a grea-

ter area and the instrument panel was improved. In the mean time construction and development work had also been concluded on a 600 cc engine with a fully synchromesh gearbox. This gearbox was actually fitted to the P 50/2. The first P 60 series was launched in autumn 1962. This car had a 600 cc engine that developed 23 hp. But the coachwork remained the same - except for a few different colours. This was officially known as the Trabant 600. Like the P 50 the P 60 was also available in an estate version, and the "Camping" version was also added, which involved a fabric sun-roof and reclining seats. The boot was enormous from the outset, with a capacity of over 400 l. Anyone who could afford a little house as well as a car carried almost everything around by Trabant. It was no rarity to see complete concrete mixers in the boot.

The Trabant was a real workhorse, swallowing everything from beer crates to concrete mixers.

Technical data for the Trabant 600

Engine	-	two-cylinder two-stroke
Capacity	-	600 cc
Performance	-	23 hp at 3,900 rpm
Max. torque	-	5.2 kpm
Compression	-	1:7.6
Fuel	-	mixture 1:33
Dynamo	-	220 w

150,000 of these Trabant 600s, which differed only slightly from the P 50, were built from 1962 to 1964.

The Trabant 601

There is no doubt that the Trabant was one of the few real stars at the time of the fall of the Berlin Wall. Who talks about the New Forum, the Round Table or the last GDR lorry, the W 50, today? After the borders were opened the plastic avalanche rolled west in millions, including a few 600s, even less 500s and the last model to be built, the 1.1, with a four-stroke engine. The Trabant 601 was seen as the symbol of East German socialism.

The Trabant 601 Limousine outside the "Teapot" in the Warnemünde district of Rostock.

In East Germany they were considered "high-quality consumer goods", and it was voted "Car of the Year" in West Germany in 1989. The very people who had called them "stinkers" and "pothole stuffers" for years now honoured them with this title. But the pampered VW, BMW, Opel or Mercedes owners could not resist the strange charm of the cosily clattering two-stroke car, whose cd value was the equivalent of that of a room divider and whose exhaust fumes could almost be charged with attempted bodily harm. While the horse-power hungry East Germans were being swindled by some of their brothers and sisters with picturesque but petrol-guzzling rust-heaps, the Trabant was in demand - at least for a time - even in Europe's no. 1 motoring country. And what joy if there was still an instruction manual or a repair handbook with it: in principle a skilled craftsman could repair every-thing on the Trabant himself, even a complete change of engine was not really a major problem.

The fact that the proud Trabi owner had to do practically everything himself in the GDR days was partly because of entirely inadequate supplies of spare parts, and partly because of a lack of workshops. Anyone who wanted good service had ideally to bring the necessary spare part as well as the appropriate baksheesh. There was no area of the GDR where contacts were more important than in car repairs and domestic jobs. This was particularly clear at the Leipzig Trade Fair. The individual exhibitors' customer service departments were the key protagonists: here you could swap a Trabant front silen-

cer for a Smalcalda hammer drill or a dynamo for 10 cases of Wernesgrüner Pilsner. Money - apart from Deutschmarks - was an uninteresting method of payment.

Typical advertising shot by Dresden photographer Christoph Czerny, whose pictures put their stamp on prospectuses and catalogues for a long period.

This car really did make history, and it was built unchanged for 26 years from 1964. Certainly a sign of continuity, but a misplaced one. The Trabant suffered the same fate as a number of GDR products as a result of political and economic constraints: when it went into production it was at the top of its class internationally, but it was never permitted any form of fundamental further development. The Exacta Varex single-lens reflex camera, the Troll motor scooter and Simson motor bikes will suffice as further examples.

When the new coachwork came into series production in 1964, the phased programme planned for the Trabant in 1959 was concluded. And this was literally true: the model really had come to the end of its development. Dr. Werner Lang, the chief design engineer responsible for the 601, had once more done good work with his team, but they had to bring off the trick of building a new car without any major investment. In fact the exterior of the 601 looked very different when compared with the 600, and seemed a much roomier vehicle, but the internal values had hardly changed at all.

In the April 1964 issue of the magazine "Der deutsche Straßenverkehr" (German Road Transport), Eberhard Preusch sang the fol-

The Trabant 601 also underwent trials in Egypt.

lowing hymn of praise: "The Trabant is scarcely recognizable with its new bodywork, although the whole underbody, engine, axles etc. have been taken over unchanged from the 600 model. The car is longer only by the dimensions of the bumpers. Nevertheless there is a lot more room inside than there was in the Trabant 600. The rear window seems to have been shifted further back than it was in the old body. Also the roof runs flat to the rear edge of the windscreen, giving more headroom for the passengers in the front. The rear seat has also been shifted a little further back, to improve leg-room for passengers in the back. But this has not made the boot any smaller, as the trapezoidal design of the rear makes maximum use of the space above the existing circular area. The Trabant 601 is at the top of the range of comparable vehicles in terms of the interior space it offers.

Another fundamental advantage of the bodywork is that the doors are fitted with wind-down windows. This means adequate ventilation in all conditions, including summer temperatures. If the windows are not open very far then wind deflector panes in the rear upper part of the windows provide largely draught-free ventilation. The inside door handles are pull devices and cannot be confused with the window winders. The doors are fastened with star locks activated by push-buttons from the outside. The key for the left-hand door simultaneously locks the press-button on the boot. The bonnet is unlocked by a pull handle as previously. Boot lid and bonnet in the new body extend almost over the full breadth of the car to the decorative strips on the wings. This means that parts placed to the sides of the engine compartment are much more accessible. It is also possible to detach the whole of the front cladding of the car including the radiator grille (in anodized aluminium) by loosening two wing nuts, to provide better access to the carburettor. The front shock absorbers are no longer fitted to the lower

View of the P 601's dashboard, showing the considerable storage space available.

A charming demonstration of how to move the back of the front seat forwards.

The P 601 estate version.

triangular pull rods, but to the transverse leaf springs. This means that they are placed higher, and thus better protected from dust, and so last longer.

The bonnet is fitted with an internal sound insulation mat, which reduces high frequency noise in particular. In addition the new cooling air deflector, which takes the cooling air downwards behind the cylinders, is coated with anti-noise filler within and without. The whole of the floor of the car including the boot has also been fitted with a sound insulation mat.

The interior trim now includes as standard two sunshades, clothes hooks, grab handles on the door columns, two ashtrays in the front and the windscreen wiper system familiar from the Wartburg. The front silencer has been modified to improve heating. It is also possible to build an additional petrol driven heater that operates independently of the engine in the boot.

The brakes have been redesigned and are now better protected against penetrating dust, and the brake blocks are now self-adjusting. Flat plug connections have replaced the screw terminals in the electrical system. They hold more reliably, even when subject to vibration, and are easy to undo. We have already reported on the centrifugal regulator for ignition control in issue 2/1964. This makes cold starting considerably easier. A temperature-compensated regulator that had already been fitted in the Trabant 600 for some time provides better battery-charging over short distances."

A journalistic masterpiece in making a great deal out of practically nothing. I was always amazed how the editors of the two weekly motoring magazines "Straßenverkehr" (Road Transport) and "Kraftfahrzeugtechnik" (Motor Vehicle Technology) managed to create such interesting issues each time. GDR vehicles were hardly noted for their innovations, and even the important import makes like Lada and Moskvich from the Soviet Union, Dacia from Romania, the Polish Polski Fiat and the Czech Skoda did not sparkle with leaps forward in development. Thus every screw, every door-handle that was different and every series part that had been developed further was presented as a major innovation. Admittedly those in the know found a suitable helping of sarcasm and self-irony between the lines, and were perfectly aware of what was going on.

But the P 601 did have some small improvements to show vis-à-vis the P 600, for example a windscreen washer fitted as standard, a larger boot and a broader bonnet. Further details were improved in subsequent years, and they were always sold as technical sensations: for example, the engine performance increased by 3 hp to 16 hp in 1969, and the heating and ventilation system was one of the items to be reworked in 1972.

The Trabant 601 was produced as a limousine and an estate car (Universal) in "standard", "special request" and "de luxe" versions. The car

The P 602 de luxe estate version.

pompously christened "de luxe" had a roof highlighted in a different colour, chromium-plated bumpers and higher quality interior finish. A special feature was the "Hycomat", which had been made since 1965. Behind this creation lay a hydro-electric clutch system that regulated clutch action automatically - the clutch was engaged by accelerating and disengaged by touching the gear lever. This was the only automatic system in the socialist block, and was particularly advantageous for the physically handicapped.

The production of the millionth Trabant was certainly a highlight event at the factory. Jubilees of this kind were celebrated with appropriate pomp. The gate through which the cars were driven into the so-called export

These advertising photographs were intended almost exclusively for foreign countries. Advertising was superfluous in the GDR, where you could be on a waiting list for ten years.

hall was covered with a gigantic paper arch with the relevant anniversary figure resplendent upon it. Then a selected worker drove - practically blind - through the paper into the hall. The signwriters had a particular task to perform when perforating the said arch: it had to tear in the most photogenic manner possible, and not fall limply all over the Trabant. But this trick always came off. The company bible "Automobilbauer einst und jetzt" (Car Builders then and now) reported the jubilee in its familiar style: "The jubilee car was due to leave the assembly belt sixteen days in advance. The Zwickau car builders had taken this upon themselves. And they kept their word. By 22 November 1973 they were there. Many employees were waiting in the sales hall in Factory II. Shortly before nine o'clock Paul Verner, a member of the Politburo and Secretary of the SED Central Committee, came into the hall; with him were Günther Kleiber, a candidate for the Politburo, deputy chairman of the Council of Ministers and Minister for General Machine, Agricultural Machine and Vehicle Construction, comrades from the Area Administration, the District Administration and the VVB (Vereinigung Volkseigener Betriebe; Organization of Nationalized Concerns) for Motor Vehicle Construction. When the finger of the clock reached nine, the coral-coloured jubilee car rolled of the belt into the hall. Paul Verner handed it over to Comrade Karl Wappler, who has worked in the factory for 36 years, as a reward for model social and specialized work." Paul Verner then spoke the usual solemn words that seem almost grotesque in retrospect: "We are all filled with particular joy because the collective of your firm, under the direction of the company party organization is among the pace-makers in our republic in striving to realize the decisions of the VIIIth Party Conference of the SED. Every one of us knows from experience that our party knows no higher interest than that of the working class and all other working people. A high tempo of development for socialist production, increased effectiveness, acceleration of scientific and technical progress and constant growth of working productivity - all these together make it possible for us to realize the principal tasks required by the VIIIth Party Conference."

The Trabant 601 on the way to the loading bay. The "white-smocked ones", so called because of their working clothes, were responsible for taking the vehicles from the final assembly stage to the good train - they were transported to the IFA delivery stores by rail.

A million cars after 15 years of production seems laughable today, alongside annual production figures of around 300,000. But when one remembers the conditions, and the prehistoric plants that were all that was available, it was a remarkable achievement.

Incidentally, celebrations involving the numbers of a particular item manufactured were not reported in the GDR media, so that ordinary citizens would not be even more annoyed about having to wait 10 to 14 years. In order to make sure that a new car was obtained every ten years at all the whole family - from the baby to grandma - was usually on the waiting list for a Trabant. Once you had managed to get hold of a car, there was no problem about financing subsequent models: a seven- or eight-year-old car could be sold for more than the price of a new one.

In 1974 the 601's specifications looked like this: the 2-cylinder two-stroke engine with induction rotary valves and an overall cubic capacity of 594.5 cc developed 26 DIN hp (30 SAE hp) at 4,200 rpm. The maximum torque was 5.5 kpm at 3,000 rpm. The mixture ratio of the fresh oil mixture lubrication was 1:30, the air-cooling fan was driven by a V-belt from the camshaft. Power was transmitted to the full synchromesh four-speed gearbox by a disc-spring clutch. The stick change on the steering column made for ease of use. The Trabant 601 was made stable to drive by a mitre-differential gearbox and propeller shaft. The integral body has a welded skeleton and the familiar Duroplast external parts. The 601 had front individual wheel suspension on suspension arms and rear individual wheel suspension on wishbones; double telescopic shock absorbers at the front and rear, rack steering and maintenance-free steering

The P 601 de luxe, with its chromium-plated bumpers, additional headlights, radio, headrests and rear side windows that could be folded open - the dream of GDR citizens in the 80s, at a price of 12,000 marks.

View of the P 601's engine compartment. The 26 litre fuel tank can be seen at the back; this was a source of danger in the case of head-on collisions in particular.

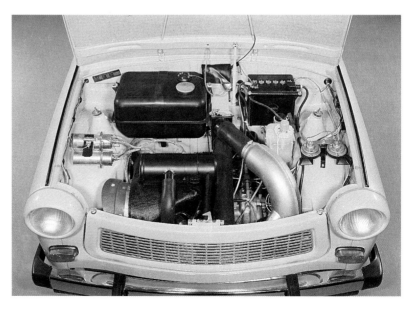

tie rods. The hydraulic foot brake worked on all four wheels and the mechanical handbrake on the rear wheels. The turning circle was 10 metres. The 601's exterior dimensions were 3,555 mm x 1,505 mm x 1,440 mm (for the Universal 3,560 mm x 1,510 mm x 1,470 mm), its unladen weight was 615 kg (650), and its payload 385 kg (390). Its top speed was 100 kph; it used 7-9 litres per 10 km and its fuel tank held 26 litres.

A whole series of improvements to its detail was developed in subsequent years; the camshaft acquired needle bearings, which made it possible to reduce the proportion of oil in the fuel mixture to 1:50, the manifold heater was improved, dual circuit brakes were fitted and the range of colours available extended. A convertible version with the sporty name "Tramp" - a civilian version of the army jeep - was added. In 1983 the Trabant acquired a 12 volt system with alternator. Fuel consumption is known to be dependent on the way the vehicle is driven in the first place.

Thus the Trabant 601 was given an accelerator pedal with a clear point of resistance three quarters of the way down. The "asphalt bubble" was also not spared the "mouse cinema", a fuel quantity indicator whose light diodes showed green, amber or red according to fuel flow. In the mid 80s the tried-and-tested leaf springs were replaced with coil springs, which was real progress in construction terms.

The jeep version of the Trabant, here being used as a "harvest helper".

A factory to produce homocinetic propeller shafts was built in Mosel near Zwickau from 1978 to 1981, in co-operation with Citroen. The factory was fully automated and had completely up-to-date technology. These new propeller shafts were used for the Trabant and also exported for Citroen and Skoda.

The Trabant at the "Acropolis Rally" in Greece.

The racers from Zwickau

Astonishingly enough, in sporting terms the Trabant played a far from insignificant part on the international rally scene from the early stages and on into the 80s. It always managed to be highly placed or to win in its class. Even on its first outing at the Semperit rally in Austria in 1959 it came first, second and third. After that 174 gold medals were won in about 200 international events. These exotic cars from the GDR were seen on the starting-line in Monte Carlo, in Greece, Finland, and all over Europe - of course always in their own class. Success was guaranteed by the drivers' skill and the proverbial reliability of the air-cooled two-stroke engines. The engines were tuned to up to 70 to 80 hp in the factory's own rally department, and reached top speeds of over 170 kph. Well-known drivers were Heinz

Feldmann and the team of Hainz Galle and Wolfgang Kießling. Rallying was very popular in the GDR, and there were often over 100,000 visitors at meetings.

Clearly this question to a broadcasting station also originated from motor sport: "Is it true that the Trabant can reach a top speed of 200 kph? Answer: in principle, yes, it just depends what height you drop it from."

The Trabant was very successful in its class in rallies in the 60s and 70s. The "cardboard racers" entered the "Monte Carlo Rally", the "1,000 Lakes Rally" in Finland and the Greek "Acropolis Rally".

Cockpit of the Rally Trabant.

Production conditions in Zwickau

Various factors detracted from Trabant manufacture in Zwickau. For example, the factory's internal hierarchy of critical employees in the VEB was so restrictive that fundamental suggestions for improving structure and organization were rarely expressed. As well as this, the party often intervened to regulate important research and development work, and even prevented new vehicles from being built. Antiquated production plant, delivery delays from the factory's suppliers, who numbered over 1,200 and shortages of material, to name the most important points, made work considerably more difficult.

Soldiers from the Soviet Army often helped with production if there were difficulties with the plan. For them it was a welcome change from the extremely strict barracks regime.

Of course a well-ordered socialist VEB was broken down into a large number of separately managed departments. There were twelve of these in the Sachsenring. As well as sections like accounts and financial control, production, basic funds business, export and internal trade, there were also interesting departments like material economy, cadre and education, social matters - to name but a few. Thus administration took up a great deal of time in

the factory, which can also be seen from the number of employees. In 1989 there were over 12,000 "workers", of whom just under one third were involved in production. Production itself was subdivided into individual manufacturing areas.

Crash test in the firm's test department

      Each department had its own head . All the departmental heads were under the director of the whole concern (Betriebsdirektor; BD), who again reported to the general director (GD) of the VEB IFA Kombinat's private car division. As in all large companies in the GDR, the VEB Sachsenring Automobilwerke Zwickau also had party, trade union and FDJ (party youth organization) management, all with permanently employed functionaries. Today the role of the party secretaries in firms is greatly over-estimated by many critics of the GDR. As a rule the state director's, in other words the BD's, word was law - in agreement with the party leadership, of which he was almost always a member. The BD was responsible for fulfilling plans and targets in every case. The BDs got their instructions from the combines, whose directors general were again "brought into line" by the responsible ministry, but also by specialist departments of the SED Central Committee and once a year by Günter Mittag personally. "Discussion with the Directors General" was intended to produce a carefully concocted summary that was published in Neues Deutschland, and also a set of instructions that was not for publication. No contradictions were tolerated, but there were nevertheless hesitant attempts at criticism, as experts were not unnaturally aware of the enormous problems. Criticism almost always came back to the person who originated it, and for this reason a number of people preferred to keep quiet and make the best of a bad job.

A symptomatic feature was the entry of graduates into the everyday world of commerce. They were often full of ideas and verve, and wanted to change a number of things that did not agree with what they had been taught at university. They were immediately put off this by the "old hands". A familiar saying was "First of all, forget everything you learnt at university". "We report successes to the top - even if there aren't any - so that we can carry on working in peace down here." With motivation like this it was not difficult to keep on in the same old rut.

The BD of VEB Sachsenring

Dr. Günter Hipp was BD, concern director, of VEB Sachsenring for many years, and he was very authoritarian. Every Party Secretary - and he survived four - had a difficult time with him. This was made more difficult by the fact that state manager Hipp was a "Candidate for the Central Committee of the SED" in the last years of the GDR, and thus above the Party Secretary in the party hierarchy, who was only a "Member of the SED Area Administration for Karl-Marx-Stadt". Thus the BD could see himself as boss of the factory twice over.

Authoritarian management often inhibited employees' creativity. As a rule their principal concern was not to make mistakes. "Only someone who doesn't work is capable of not making mistakes" was a popular saying in the GDR. There was considerable camouflage in middle management in particular. But their were sectional and divisional managers and also departmental heads who were prepared to speak their mind, and who suggested solutions. But they were the exception.

In the Monday management meetings at VEB Sachsenring, in which the departmental heads were also involved, the complete dilemma was clear. On the one hand there were constant demands for increased production, improves quality and lower costs, on the other hand completely inadequate resources for urgently needed refurbishment and investment. It was not until the early 80s that automation and the first industrial robots put an end to the medieval production conditions. Management meetings often went round in circles because of the afore-mentioned inconsistency between demands made on the company and its real implementation capacity.

Production results were often talked up. There was also the well-tried device of plan correction, which was always used when the original plan could not be fulfilled. Today this is probably known as "annual target adjustment".

Very few people enjoyed working under this constant pressure - "I hope you've not done anything wrong." But we should also not forget that the BD, the director of the firm, was subject to constraints as well, which in the case of a "high-quality consumer product" like the Trabant often came "right from the top". Orders from the combine, the Ministry or the Central Committee had to be implemented with complete rigour. The "State Managers" and above all the BD were responsible for this. Incidentally, the Party Secretary was not involved in the weekly management meetings. All the departmental heads were members of the SED.

The authoritarian management style, which actually ran counter to socialist collective thinking, was the exception rather than the rule for major concerns and combines. Obviously this was seen as the only way of keeping workers on the go. In the VEB Sachsenring as well, there were committed car-builders but also many familiar figures - in management in particular - who sat it out and made sure they'd got their retirement homes organized. It is quite a different thing to say that firms could have been managed more humanely and less strictly. The VEB Sachsenring was certainly not bad training for those people who made the leap into a new career under market-economy conditions.

Production

Production in the VEB Sachsenring was broken down into individual production sections, which the Trabi ran through from production to delivery. These sections were organized as follows:

Body-shells before further processing. The Trabant was completed in three phases, and transport inside the factory was by lorry.

Manufacturing section 1 - compression moulding

Here cotton was mixed with phenolic resin to produce the Duroplast material. This mixture was then moved to large presses in which the material was heated and compressed to produced the Duroplast parts for the bodywork. These parts were subsequently cut to the correct size.

Machine for mixing cotton and resin for the Duroplast.

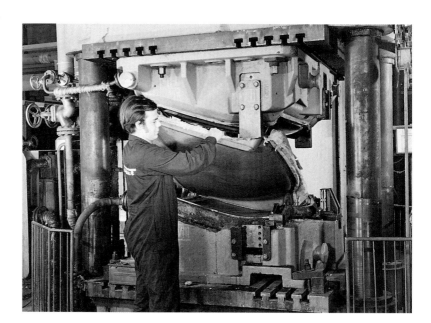

Taking a complete Duroplast section out of the press.

The Duroplast parts were cut to size with band-saws after pressing.

Cutting a Duroplast bonnet flap.

Manufacturing section 2 - assembling the body-shell

Welding the parts of the body and manufacturing the brakes were central to this production phase. From the mid 80s industrial robots were increasingly used at this stage. Nevertheless numerous spot welds had to be done by hand, which was physically very difficult work.

The sheet steel skeleton was welded and sanded at the body-shell assembly stage.

Welding machine at the body-shell assembly stage.

Spot-welding at the body-shell assembly stage.

Manufacturing section 3 - body covering and painting

Here the body shells went through an electrophoretic immersion bath and the Duroplast cladding was subsequently fitted. After that the Trabi was painted. Robots were also used here from 1985.

Electrophoretic immersion bath for the body-shell, which was made of sheet steel and then covered with Duroplast.

Spraying robot painting the bodywork.

Manufacturing section 6 -
private car gearbox manufacture and metal processing

This was the electroplating shop, along with gearbox part manufacturing and gear-box fitting

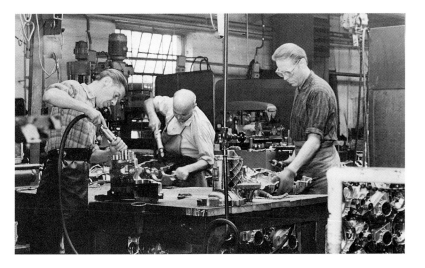

Here the sheet steel bodywork has already had the Duroplast cladding fitted. The process was not in fact fully automated, it's just that this photograph was taken in a break.

Gearbox construction workbench

Manufacturing section 7 - Mosel painting and final assembly

The last of the manufacturing sections was established in Mosel near Zwickau in 1989, immediately adjacent to the propeller shaft plant. West German and western European firms were involved in creating a high mechanized or automated paint and final assembly shop, which was already tailored to the Trabant 1.1 with four-stroke engine.

Completed bodies before final assembly

Once the body had got here it went through several phases, from sub-assembly to insertion of the glass to the "wedding", the union of body and engine. Because of the many technical and technological inadequacies due to lack of investment the rejection rate was very high. Additional work was constantly needed. For examples, the mechanics often had to work on doors and locks with hammers.

"Wedding" in the final assembly phase: body and engine are fitted together.

Turning the body in the final fitting phase was a considerable relief. This obviated difficult overhead work.

Manufacturing section 10 - parts manufacture

Small parts like steering racks, brake cylinders, chassis and steering parts were made in this section.

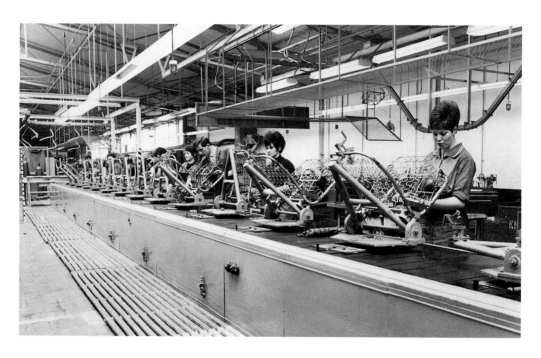

Workers in the seat manufacturing section were mainly women.

Manufacturing section 11 - sheet metal pressing

Here all the pressed metal parts lie doors, side sections and wheel cases were made. Capacity was increased in the mid 80s when a new pressing shop was built with new, electronically controlled large-scale presses.

View of the sheet metal press.

The new pressing shop with modern technology produced in the GDR went into production in the mid 80s.

Manufacturing section 13 - Mosel propeller shaft manufacturing plant

Propeller shafts were produced here for the German car industry and for export from 1986, in co-operation with Citroen.

A short-supply economy and how its effects could be covered up

The old VEB Sachsenring sheet metal press

Even such an important producer of consumer goods as the Trabant manufacturer, whose products had a direct influence on the mood of the population, ran the gamut of unpredictability within the daily production process: antiquated machines and belts packed up, there were scarcely any spare

parts, supplies of engines from Chemnitz dried up, the Universal bodies from Chemnitz did not arrive in time, there was no sheet steel, quality was often inadequate, urgent investment was not possible, periods of failure became longer and longer, material consumption was too high, there were increasingly differences in stock-taking figures, a departmental mentality was felt more and more and so on and so forth!

Examples could go on ad infinitum. This showed clearly what the real problem of a socialist command economy was: the plan was the law, but it usually had feet of clay, as the correct basis was not there, in terms of either materials or money. Figures were plucked out of the air to lead people to believe in an imaginary increase, projects were taken on that were substantiated by nothing at all, profits made by the firm disappeared into the bottomless pit of "social policy", and there were insufficient funds for investment. And the average worker had long since lost his or her zest and come to terms with the realities of the situation in a resigned fashion - anyway it did not seem that anything could be changed. People swam with the current, remained inconspicuous, and so everything went its "socialist way".

But the "creative urge" and the "mass initiative" that were so often invoked fell by the wayside. Attempts were made to use unviable methods like the "personal creative plan", the "collective creative plan", "socialist work schools", "fund returns", the "Schwedt initiative", "title struggle" (socialist work collective) and similar paper tigers to breathe life into "socialist competition".

Under the "personal creative plan", individual workers committed themselves to fulfilling individual plans, to working innovatively (today: company suggestions), to increasing the effectiveness of their work, to lowering costs summed up under ANG, i.e. "Ausschuß, Nacharbeit, Garantie" (Rejects, further work, guarantee). They also committed themselves to supporting the PSR (Plan der sozialistischen Rationalisierung; socialist rationalization plan), and other projects that were scarcely open to any sort of check. Then again, the "Schwedt Initiative" meant, in brief, saving workers by rationalization and then using them somewhere else. But in practice jobs and workers were just pushed to and fro without making the working process any more effective. This initiative was named after the Schwedt petro-chemical combine in which it originated, one of the largest companies in the GDR.

Some of these methods could also perhaps have been successful in the conditions had been right and employees had had a chance to make creative contributions. But people were afraid to analyse the status quo too deeply - the results would have been too demoralizing. Weary of slogans and of "economic agitation and propaganda", which as "socialist production propaganda" fell into my sphere of work, everyone was looking for a private niche.

P50 bodies having their panels fitted

Car-making as confidential information

The history of motor car development in the GDR is also symptomatic of the system. Quite apart from the problems that have already been mentioned, there were not just costings and initial thinking about new cars, but also entirely new vehicles that were developed to the prototype stage.

The Trabant itself was always just a further development of the DKW. Later, in the mid 60s, it was antiquated both technically and structurally. And precisely at this point its potential successor was in the starting blocks . . . For in fact the Zwickau design engineers under Dr. Werner Lang had been discontented with the present vehicle for some time. Thus various versions were produced, laboriously and shielded from the public gaze; they reflected the most up-to-date technology and were actually at the apogee in terms of structure and body design.

The P 603 was the most perfect. Its features included a four-stroke engine, automatic transmission and a fastback body. In appearance it anticipated later VW and Opel models. Astonishingly the Wankel engine was also tried out in Zwickau, and joint research into the ceramic engine was also undertaken jointly with the Zwickau engineering college.

So there was no doubt that the technicians were able to develop a competitive car. And the highly qualified specialist workers would also have been able to produce such a vehicle. But other projects were at the top of the Politburo's list, and as there was actually no chance that funds would be available, private car development in the GDR fell by the wayside.

There was another shot at a new car in the late sixties. The "Rat für Gegenseitige Wirtschaftshilfe" (Mutual Economic Assistance Council; RGW) was intended to co-ordinate the economies of the socialist states. Thus Hungary was supposed to take over bus production (Ikarus), Czechoslovakia was intended to take over lorries and trams (Skoda, Tatra), and the GDR's responsibilities would include machine tool manufacture. Skoda and VEB Sachsenring were also to produce a car jointly as part of this co-operative scheme. The Czechs were responsible for the engine and the braking system and the East Germans were to develop the body, the gearbox etc. This new model was again to use an all-steel body instead of the Duroplast cladding.

This project, the P 610, was also developed to the ready-for-driving stage. But the desolate economic position, constantly rising costs and ever-increasing problems with time meant that series production was unthinkable. Politburo member Günter Mittag in particular constantly blocked initiatives by the Zwickau car-builders. Even though he had personal experience of the levels of technology at VEB Sachsenring, the last time on 30 June 1986, the urgently needed funds were not granted. Other branches of the industry, like chemicals and electronics, for example, had priority.

The Zwickau prototypes were hidden in a cellar in the test department, when it was not decreed that they should be destroyed for political reasons. The PS 603, which would certainly have been a hit, met the former fate. After November 1989 even old-established Sachsenring workers were amazed at what would have been possible when they found the cars. Today some of these unique specimens can be found in the August-Horch-Museum in Zwickau.

Social and cultural facilities in the VEB

The car factory in Zwickau was not just a place where a large number of employees worked, it also supplied them with a large number of additional services. The car-builders often spent their leisure time with colleagues, using facilities set up by the firm; they pursued their hobbies and worked on projects together.

Social politics in the factory

The S 4000, which was developed from the H 3A, outside one of VEB Sachsenring's first workers' housing co-operative (AWG) blocks.

Large firms in the GDR had their own medical, cultural and social facilities as a rule. The VEB Sachsenring had a major department of social politics. It dealt with matters including accommodation, holidays, social needs and intellectual and cultural life.

The VEB Sachsenring also had an AWG (Arbeiterwohnungsbaugenossenschaft; workers' housing co-operative). Members were able to shorten the waiting time for a home considerably. In all the GDR housing co-ope-

ratives members had to pay co-operative dues and also put in a quota of hours of work, dependent on the size of the future accommodation, on building sites or doing refurbishment work. The number of hours varied between 400 and 700, and they were mainly put in at the weekend or in holidays. The advantage was that workers got homes this way after a waiting period of about two years, which was short for the time. Of course the homes were heavily subsidised. Living-room, bedroom, bathroom and kitchen cost barely 50 marks in monthly rental, and even with two bedrooms the rent was well

under 100 marks. Of course this has to be related to wages and salaries: a skilled worker earned between 800 and 1,200 marks net, a section manager about 1,200 marks. Nevertheless Zwickau, with its completely antiquated building stock, had thousands of people looking for homes, and new building in the districts of Eckersbach and Neu-Planitz made very little difference to this. Housing applications from young families with children went to the top of the list, and "good connections" played an important part at that time.

      The firm had lavish medical facilities. It had its own out-patients' clinic for the benefit of all its employees. As everywhere in the GDR, all

View of the common-room in the apprentices' home. Many of the trainees came from Mecklenburg and were accommodated in a boarding-school in Zwickau.

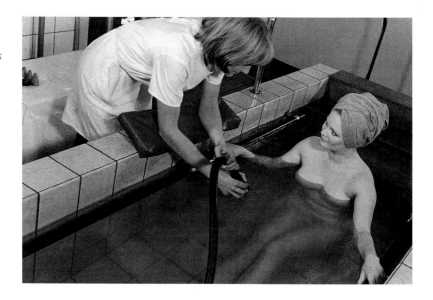

*Photograph adver-
tising therapeutic
facilities in the firm's
out-patients' clinic.*

examinations, treatments and prescriptions were free. The clinic had general practitioners and three dentists, but also specialists in neurology, orthopaedics, urology, dermatology, gynaecology, surgery, internal medicine, ophthalmology and hygiene at work. It also had a lab, a sauna and a dental workshop, alongside an X-ray department and numerous therapy facilities. As well as this every section of the factor had departmental doctors.

*Factory crèche in
the 60s.*

As 90 per cent of women in the GDR worked, crèche facilities - for children up to 3 - and kindergartens - for children from four to six - were very important. The VEB Sachsenring had a range of children's facilities, and they were practically free: only a nominal monthly charge was payable. 2,100 children used them, but they were prepared for "socialist" life.

The firm's Kulturhaus - House of Culture - played an important part in the "intellectual and social life" of the "brigades", or teams of workers. Party and trade union events took place in its hall, which seated about 800, conferences for "innovators" and "promoters of intensification", but also family dances, concerts, women's day celebrations, departmental evenings and "competition winners' balls". 16 "people's art circles" also worked in the club-house. Anyone who wanted to could pursue hobbies after work: photography, dancing, amateur drama, painting, carving and many other things were possible, all with expert direction. The firm's trade union organization directed and financed the Kulturhaus. Siegfried Voitel directed it for many years, and was well-known even outside the local community. He was committed to a very attractive programme and to the people's art circle.

The factory had fully equipped facilities for children. This photograph shows the kindergarten.

The "Silver Swan" dancing circle was one of 16 popular art circles in the factory's "Kulturhaus".

The best people's art collectives in the country met at the GDR "workers' festival", and the Sachsenringers often won gold medals there.

The Sachsenring Employees' Sports Association (Betriebssportgemeinschaft; BSG) had a good reputation well beyond Zwickau. Its footballers were successful in the first division and provided many players for the nat-

The VEB Sachsenring choir appeared at factory events and in the region.

ional team, the boxers, tennis, table-tennis and handball players, and the skittlers were at the top at regional level and provided the established sports clubs with some fierce competition. The party was interfered massively in sport as well. The former administrative are of Karl-Marx-Stadt (Chemnitz) had three football clubs, who played in the first division, the highest in the GDR: FC Karl-Marx-Stadt, BSG Wismut Aue and indeed BSG Sachsenring Zwickau. The first-mentioned club enjoyed special support from the SED area administration, and key players from other clubs had to be "delegated" there. Practically every Sachsenring employees supported the firm's team - and its was much more popular than the Karl-Marx-Stadt club.

But popular sport was rated just as highly as competitive sport. There was an annual firm sports day, and everyone could play a sport without being exposed to the stress of competitions.

The firm also provided and financed holidays. Employees could use many VEB holiday facilities in pleasant rural areas. 14 days including full board cost 240 marks per person. Sachsenringers enjoyed travelling to the "brother country" of Hungary.

Both the factory and the trade union were particularly concerned with trainees. Many apprentices were housed in the firm's own boarding-

The BSG Sachsenring Zwickau was the longest-serving team in the GDR first division until it was relegated. Its best-known player was Jürgen Croy, who often played in goal for the national team. This photograph shows an incident from the Wismut Aue - Sachsenring game, taken by the then director of the company's photographic circle Frank Kruczynski, who was a successful sports photographer.

View of the sports hall in the factory's own vocational school, which offered various training courses - fitter, electrician, welder, painter, maintenance mechanic, shorthand typist, cook etc. - and appropriate specialist training.

house. The VEB Sachsenring vocational school trained them, and the apprentice often spent their leisure time together at events organized by the Sport and Technology Association (Gesellschaft für Sport und Technik; GST) or the FDJ.

Of course all these activities fulfilled an important function in developing a certain feeling of togetherness among colleagues. Despite being fed up with politics and resisting the party's constantly repeated slogans people liked meeting in the collective, the sports club or the people's art circle to go to the theatre, have "brigade" evenings or Christmas festivities.

However, leisure activities were also subject to a curious "quality control" system. Once a year the so-called L-presentation on "intellectual and cultural life" had to be made to the firm's director (L). I twice had the pleasure of being in charge of this. The presentation summed up the past year's leisure activities and suggested an approach for the next year. As was generally the case with summaries and statistics a great deal of rounding off upwards went on. This applied to "brigade" events, theatre visits, skittle evenings, participants in the firm's sports day and also the number of "brigade" diaries kept, or visits to museums and memorials. I placed a quotation from the esteemed Soviet writer Daniil Granin from his novel "The Painting" at the head of one of these presentations, which was couched in the usual party and trade union jargon. Granin was reproaching commercial functionaries with not being sufficiently interested in culture. Result: the presentation was rejected and had to be revised. The production director repre-

Many young people in the GDR were in the GST as well as the FDJ. The GST provided various working groups (gliding, model-building etc.). It was also responsible for "pre-military training". The photograph shows apprentices from VEB Sachsenring being trained to shoot with small-bore sub-machine-guns.

senting the director of the enterprise felt personally attacked by this "dissident stuff".

Despite the desolate economic situation the VEB Sachsenring like other firms in the GDR offered its workers completely comprehensive, free medical, social and cultural facilities. In retrospect it is a mystery how it was possible to guarantee all these services for so many decades.

The Trabi as a holiday companion.

Of battleships and white horses - the party and VEB Sachsenring

Of the firm's 12,000 employees 2,300 were members of the SED. The "workers' party" has long been the white-collar party in the Sachsenring factory.

Party work in the car factory

Departmental party meetings and meetings for apprentices - the latter merely an agit-prop event - took place once a month outside working hours. The departmental meetings dealt with current events in world politics, GDR politics, long-winded and mantra-like evaluations of plenary session of the Central Committee, speeches by Politburo members and at congresses; but they also dealt with plan fulfilment in the factory, staffing problems, voting and opinions. Things often became heated, because contrary to predominant ideas the party meeting did offer an opportunity to criticize existing shortcomings or to complain about the way in which management behaved. Admittedly most comrades were faithful supporters and just dosed through the two hours. It was always the same people who were involved in the arguments, and there were definitely not enough critical voices. Everyone was delighted when someone came up with a reproach, pointed out deficiencies or criticized certain kinds of behaviour - but support was scarcely to be expected. However, criticism voiced in this context was not held against those who voiced it.

Task force training
in the late 50s.

The director of the VEB was a member of APO (the local party organization) L just as I was, and we had some very interesting clashes. (The L stood for the factory director's department with its staff departments.) His function alone meant that he had to put forward the official line, while I could be the "voice of the people". Of course it didn't make any difference, but at least I had a safety valve . . .

The APO's annual programme for action was a masterly achievement. A few quotations from the last party conference, some extracts from current planning tasks, several commitments to working even more effectively, to provide better quality, to reduce ANG costs, to fulfil the PSR - all well shaken up and topped with a promise to recruit new members for the Society for German-Soviet Friendship (GDSF) and to pay solidarity contributions punctually - and that was it.

The factory's party management and the organs concerned with this were built up in teams:

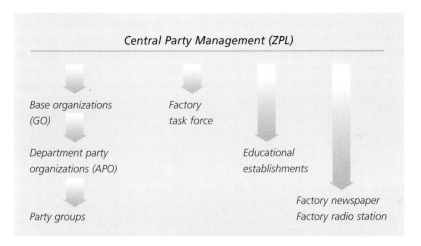

Central Party Management (ZPL)

Base organizations (GO)

Factory task force

Department party organizations (APO)

Educational establishments

Party groups

Factory newspaper Factory radio station

The following were members of the central party leadership: the party secretary, two deputies, the economic policy secretary, the GO secretaries, the chairman of the factory trade union committee, the FDJ secretary, the factory director and comrades from the departments. The last factory party secretary but one once described his status as follows: "The factory director is the wise old owl, I know nothing." In other words: the factory director was totally in control.

Otherwise the party stewed in its own juice to a large extent. The functionaries tried to influence all the employees, but that was an absolutely hopeless enterprise. The same people always met at discussions and conferences organized by the party, and the collectives had very little political clout, especially as the principal task of the factory's party organization was to make sure that the plan was fulfilled. The factory newspaper and the factory radio station were "organs of the party leadership". Their content was also correspondingly wearisome. Usually readers had the privilege of casting

An early example of design for the Mayday procession: the celebration car for the Mayday demonstration on 1 May 1958, with a design symbolizing the merger of the two firms VEB Sachsenring (formerly Horch) and VEB Automobilwerk Zwickau (formerly Audi) to form VEB Sachsenring Automobilwerke Zwickau.

an eye over the usual reports of success from the "brigades" and touched-up balance sheets.

An annual high-spot was the work of the factory's "May Committee", which always met in January under the chairmanship of the party secretary. Its members included the GO secretaries and managers or departmental directors who were responsible for organizing the procession on 1 May. There were also representatives of the trade union, the FDJ, the GDSF, the Klubhaus director and other functionaries.

My department was mainly responsible for preparing and carrying out the Mayday celebrations. It included the visual agitation group (lettering experts and graphic artists), the factory photographic group, the factory press officer and the colleague responsible for "production propaganda". The last-named individual was known throughout the factory. Mayday released reserves to him that you would scarcely have thought possible. He presented the first draft of the "Marching Book" to the Mayday committee as early as February. This was effectively a screenplay for the part of the May demonstration designed by VEB Sachsenring.

About 7,000 of the firm's employees took part in this annual procession, which set off from the factory to march through the town. There it was joined by other enterprises, who then marched on to the VIP stand. The Marching Book fixed the individual "images", which were always linked to a particular theme, like for example "Using industrial robots", "We are fulfilling the decrees of the VIIIth Party Conference", "Our balance-sheet is sound", "Successful social policies" or even "Friendship with the Soviet Union". Every image had a decorated lorry, illustrating the theme with placards, models or even a genuine industrial robot. In addition there were about 180 banners with figures from the plan and slogans and numerous "waving elements" in the form of little flags, artificial flowers or balloons.

76

It was not easy to organize all the materials needed for the procession given the permanent shortages. The Marching Book was discussed and changed at Mayday committee meetings, slogans were formulated, the course of events fixed, the necessary personnel made available and political and ideological preparations made in the working collectives. The intention was to offer powerful figures from the district, who would graciously allow the procession to file past them, an image of perfect unity.

In the course of all this there were some very silly suggestions, usually coming from the factory's trade union chairman. For example, he wanted the factory director to parade before his fellow-workers on a "white horse". On the occasion of the 60th anniversary of the October Revolution he suggested that a model of the battleship "Aurora", which started the October Revolution by opening fire on the Winter Palace in St. Petersburg should join the procession on a low-loader. The model would then fire cannon-shots on passing the VIP stand. He had an even more wild and woolly idea on the occasion of the "40th anniversary of liberation" in 1985 to use Soviet solidarity with the VEB to get hold of one of the legendary T 34s - the Red Army's Second World War tank - and to let it rattle along at the head of the procession. While the members of the Mayday committee practically burst with suppressed laughter, the party secretary had great difficulty in talking his comrade trade union chairman out of this idea.

As well as this the part organized a number of conferences and formed various working parties and committees. Most employees found the GO secretaries' political zeal a source of mild amusement. "Party committee conferences were held at regular intervals and were concerned with the same problems as every management group: it was all about fulfilling the key requirements of the plan, problems like poor quality, increasing ANG costs, worker shortages, science and technology and investment.

Thus for example the factory director announced the following figures for planned investment at the party committee conference on 13 January 1988:

- *19 million foreign currency marks for final assembly*
- *87 million foreign currency marks for the paintshop*
- *30 million foreign currency marks for welding equipment*
- *4 million foreign currency marks for a test bed*
- *20 million foreign currency marks for a transfer production line*
- *13 million foreign currency marks for new tools*

Walter Ulbricht im Werk

High-level visit in Zwickau

State and party dignitaries often stopped in Zwickau to find out about progress in the car industry. The visit by Günter Mittag, Secretary for Economic
Affairs in the Politburo and Deputy Chairman of the GDR State Council
in June 1986 is a textbook example of how leading comrades went to a
great deal of trouble to give the impression of a perfect world "at the grass-
roots". His visit took place on the 40th anniversary of referendum on the
expropriation of former armaments firms in Saxony, which was described
above. Three months before the visit a factory working party was formed
under the chairmanship of the factory manager. Its members included all
departmental managers, who had to make sure that the "highly-placed visitor" went back to Berlin with the best possible impressions of the Zwickau
factory.

The factory security department was of course involved in the preparations,
and so were the maintenance department, which was responsible for build-

ing work, urgently needed superficial improvements, building a VIP stand and cleaning production areas, and also the production department itself, whose employees had to bring workshops that were to be included in the visit up to scratch. The social department organized all supply aspects, right down to "Margon", which was Mittag's preferred brand of mineral water, and they were also commissioned to write a paper summing up "improvements in working and living conditions". The technology department was to report on current development work, the Klubhaus was to design the conference rooms and laid on the factory orchestra. The public relations department had to perform a number of tasks by the day of the visit: the "visual agitation" - banners, wall newspapers, information panels - had to be designed ad hoc, an exhibition set up and press material provided. They also prepared an album containing a large number of photographs presenting the VEB's social policy and the modern propeller shaft company.

Of course the working party also included the party secretary, the trade union chairman and the FDJ secretary. Later representatives of the SED district and leadership were included. At first meetings took place every two weeks, and almost daily in the final phase.

The subjects mentioned on the exhibition panels presented to Mittag make it perfectly clear how much things have been dressed up:

Panel 1 - *Successful use of robots*

Panel 2 - *CAD/CAM-solutions for construction/technology and production*

Panel 3 - *Effect of construction using rationalization measures in the factory, moving away from NSW imports (these were imports from "non-socialist economic areas")*

Panel 4 - *Increase in production to 165,000 private cares by 1988, restructuring the factory as a bodywork and assembly plant with a production increase to 175,000 p.a.*

Panel 5 - *comparison of drive units: old (two-stroke) - new (VW four-stroke)*

Panel 6 - *Fulfilling principal figures*

Panel 7 - *The Mosel propeller-shaft factory*

Panel 8 - *Results and obligations arising from the XIth SED party conference*

Panel 9 - *Planned investment*

Panel 10 - *Plans for 1987*

Of course only successes and planned projects were listed here - the perfect world of VEB Sachsenring. There was also an exhibition of the range of cars, including old models like the DKW F 8, F 9, P 70.

The GDR paid particular attention to banners and slogans. It was no different when Günter Mittag came to Sachsenring: banners were refurbished, the "production line of the best" was redesigned, new "visual elements" were put up, factory signs varnished, corners that had been dirty for years were swept, halls cleaned. I well remember a particular weekend's work: the guest was due to meet about 2,000 factory employees in the bodywork shop. Workers put up an enormous stand, flanked by a banner proclaiming "What the people's hand creates should be the people's own". As the visit was on a Monday, all departments and the stand were inspected on Saturday. Suddenly the factory director decided that the banner, which was anyway 10 metres long and 60 cm high. I was given the job of making one that was twice as big by Sunday evening. And so I forced myself into one of the firm's cars on the Saturday and drove to the VEB's signwriters, who lived about 20 km away - to their home, or rather to their weekend plot of land. Fortunately I managed to persuade them to make the new banner on the Sunday.

Another important visitor: "Our minister, Comrade Günter Kleiber, finds out about the TR 10" (original caption).

Then on 30 June 1986 at 10 a.m. the moment came: Günter Mittag was welcomed by the 1st Secretary of the SED District and the factory bosses, surrounding by "jubilant" apprentices with "portable elements" and employees who had been drummed up for the occasion. First of all a task force unit filed past him, accompanied by the "Yorck March". After that there was a meeting in the Klubhaus. The factory director explained the current situation at VEB Sachsenring and made some comments about the exhibition. There was then a tour of the bodywork shop. Selected workers were waiting at selected stopping points to tell Comrade Mittag about their achievements and the technical progress that had been made. These contribution had of course been carefully prepared.

But there were some spontaneous statements that could not be prevented by the local state security officials who were present or by comrades from the factory. For example, one female worker complained vociferously about poor supplies in the town, especially of potatoes. The blushing Party Secretary assured her that he would do something about it immediately (and he did).

The meeting with 2,000 Sachsenringers and workers from other forms in Zwickau followed the tried-and-tested pattern: first of all the district secretary welcomed the visitors. A skilled worker from the factory spoke "on behalf of the workers of the town", and reported on wonderful results and projects. Then it was Mittag's turn; he made one of the usual

agitprop speeches, promised help and support with work in the future and sang a hymn of praise for the policies of the party and the region. Then he was presented with the album of photographs mentioned above, and asked to pass it on to General Secretary Erich Honecker. Then there was lunch with 50 selected workers. The visit was over at 2.30 p.m. In the mean time there was of course time enough for Mittag to criticize the state leadership and the party leadership of the VEB vigorously and to demand with impeccable logic that decrees be carried out. The fact that conditions simply did not allow this was quietly ignored by all present . . .

The factory liked showing its techno-logy to meritorious citizens of the GDR: Sigmund Jahn, the GDR's first pilot cos-monaut, during his tour at ZMMM 1982.

Epilogue: the last Trabant

There came a point at which even the Politburo of the SED Central Committee realized that the Trabant, which was hopelessly antiquated and took too long to produce could only be rescued by modernization. By now even the GDR's rulers could no longer ignore the fact that the two-stroke engine was not appropriate to the times, either in terms of performance or the exhaust gases it produced. Pressure from export partners, who took delivery of just under a quarter of the vehicles produced, became increasingly strong.

Relatives in the West and Western television also kept GDR citizens informed about the current state of the motor car industry. Small numbers of imports, like 10,000 VW Golfs and quite a few Mazdas showed where indigenous production stood: in the automotive Middle Ages.

The Sachsenringers had shown in the 50s that they could reach European standards. But a clapped-out economy and bureaucrats who were opposed to progress inhibited development. Now the connection had to be made within a very few years. The Politburo made appropriate decisions in 1983 and 1984. These were the resolution of 14 June 1983 and that of the Committee of the Council of Ministers of 23 June about "problems and measures for the rapid increase of private car production up to 1985 and afterwards", and the Politburo resolution of 9 October 1984 on "realizing the engine concept for the Wartburg and Trabant private cars". The internal name for the latter was "AA" - "Antriebsaggregat" (drive unit). Of course these resolutions came far too late. By this time the Trabant was a museum piece, a vintage car. Finally a new engine factory was built in co-operation with VW in what was then Karl-Marx-Stadt for the planned production of a new engine. Building was due to start in 1984, and engine production could start as soon as the factory was completed.

The careful opening-up of the Soviet Union after the death of Leonid Brezhnev had a not inconsiderable influence on more open allusions to shortcomings. Careful criticism was voiced even under Yuri Andropov, and there was a breath of freshness in the air. The Soviets started to identify political and economic shortcomings and to blame functionaries who had seemed untouchable until then. The "Presse der Sowjetunion", the organ of the "Society for German-Soviet Friendship", which mainly carried contributions from Soviet publications, was transformed from being excruciatingly boring into sought-after reading matter. Also the "Sputnik", which came into being under Gorbachov and was actually banned in the GDR for a time revealed faults and shortcomings that were much the same as those in the GDR.

Faced with this cautious change in the atmosphere warning voices started to be raised within the East German economy. It took some time before there was any reaction, as criticism of this kind almost reached "party and government" in a heavily filtered and toned-down form.

Finally a programme was published - with the necessary funding - for modernizing the whole of the GDR motor industry between 1987 and 1990. The Trabant was at last to be produced with a four-stroke engine, as decided as early as 1984. In autumn 1989 the moment came: the Trabant 1.1

with the VW Polo's four-cylinder four-stroke engine built under licence was available to be launched before an astonished public, though externally practically nothing had changed: the new engine was hidden under the old Trabant's body.

The new Trabant was presented in a contribution to the GDR television "Transport Magazine" in early September 1989. I drove the "new" car, and I can still see the horrified faces of the Lada drivers and those of the West Germans on the Transit route near Michendorf as a Trabant hammered

Trabant 1.1 Universal with 1.1 l four-stroke Volkswagen engine, called the "mummy with a pacemaker".

Technical data for the Trabant 1.1

Engine	-	four-cylinder four-stroke in-line engine
Bore	-	75 mm
Stroke	-	59 mm
Cubic capacity	-	1043 cc
Compression	-	9.5
Performance	-	40 hp at 5300 rpm
Cooling	-	water
Carburettor	-	downdraft carburettor
Clutch	-	single-disk dry clutch
Gearbox	-	four-speed synchromesh
Shift	-	column shift
Brakes	-	front disk brakes, rear drum brakes
Overall length	-	3555 mm
Overall width	-	1504 mm
Overall height	-	1437 mm
Unladen weight	-	700 kg
Payload	-	385 kg
Maximum speed	-	125 kph
Consumption-		7-9 l/100 km

past them at the crazy speed - for it - of 140 kph. The film had to be passed by the economics department of the Politburo before it was broadcast, which unexpectedly caused no difficulties.

By 30 November 1989, in other words until after the fall of the Berlin Wall, 830 Trabant 1.1s were built in parallel with the two-stroke version. The first Trabant 1.1 went to the dispatch department on 14 May 1990. On 21 May 1990 the 3 millionth Trabant, a 1.1, came off the production line in the new assembly plant in Mosel. The first VW Polo was assembled from components there at the same time. Finally political events caught up with VEB Sachsenring as they had with the whole of the GDR. On 26 June 1990, at about 2 p.m., the factory stopped producing the Trabant 601. Only a few Universals were produced after this. A few desperate attempts to reposition the 1.1 on the market, the "Tramp" leisure vehicle, for example, came to nothing. On 30 April 1991 the long and distinguished story of car production in Zwickau came to an end for the time being.

Today, seven years on, it is hard to draw up a balance-sheet. Observers tend to mock the technical inadequacies of the vehicles and the plant. Those who were involved know about all the constraints, shortages and restrictions that surrounded production of a car that was every family's dream at the time. It would be worth devoting an entire book to how we had to improvise, negotiate, swap, bribe, and put pressure on the SED area leadership. Methods were used to secure daily production that were in fact illegal. Sometimes the factory

Visually scarcely anything had happened to the Trabant 1.1

had no sheet metal, then their was a shortage of welding electrodes. But the Trabant was a coveted object that could be swapped. It didn't always have to be a whole car, a foam steering-wheel or a door seal could work little miracles on their own. The fact that antiquated plant and machines produced a product that could be driven at all is due to the ability and improvisational skills of about 12,000 Sachsenringers; Western European journalists who visited the Zwickau factory in large numbers after November 1989 were absolutely astonished.

The Trabant 1.1 Tramp was one of the last attempts to rescue production in Zwickau after November 1989. The 1.1 was short for the 1.1 l four-stroke engine produced using VW know-how in Karl-Marx-Stadt (now Chemnitz).

Glossary

Language in the GDR was full of "socialist" coinages and a large number of abbreviations. To give the reader a sense of the ideas used in this book they are listed and decoded here.

ALB	Arbeits- und Lebensbedingungen (living and working conditions) - continual improvement of the ALB was a noble ideal in the GDR.
ANG	Ausschuß, Nacharbeit, Garantie (rejects, extra work, guarantee) - costs influenced by workers, which were to be kept as low as possible.
APO	Abteilungsparteiorganisation (departmental party organization) - party organization subordinate to the ZPL
BD	Betriebsdirektor (factory director) - the state director of a concern
BGL	Betriebsgewerkschaftsleitung (factory trade union leadership)
BKV	Betriebskollektivvertrag (factory collective contract) - agreement between the factory management and the BGL
BPO	Betriebsparteiorganisation (factory party organization)
Brigade	Team of workers, particularly in the production field
BSG	Betriebssportgemeinschaft (factory sport association) - the BSG provided the workers at VEB Sachsenring with sporting events and facilities. Sports courses could be attended for a contribution of 1.20 marks per month.
Duroplast	a mixture of cotton waste and phenolic resin developed especially for bodywork construction

FB	Fertigungsbereich (manufacturing department) - production section within the VEB
FDGB	Freier Deutscher Gewerkschaftsbund (Free German Trade Union Federation) - the GDR trade union association
FDJ	Freie Deutsche Jugend (Free German Youth) - the GDR youth organization

Wir helfen den Steinkohlenkumpels bei der Planerfüllung

GD	Generaldirektor (general director) - immediate superior of the BD, director of the combine	*Car workers helped out in the Zwickau coal mines.*
GDSF	Gesellschaft für deutsch-sowjetische Freundschaft (Society for German-Soviet Friendship)	
GO	Grundorganisation (basic organization) of the SED - subordinate to the ZPL	

GST	Gesellschaft für Sport und Technik (Society for Sport and Technology) - socialist mass organization with a pre-military character for young people interested in sport and technology
GWW	Gelenkwellenwerk (propeller shaft factory)
Hycomat	automatic clutch developed for the Trabant

With this P601 the Zwickau car builders fulfil the 1971-1975 Five Year Plan.

IFA	Industrieverwaltung Fahrzeugbau (Industrial Vehicle Construction Administration) - umbrella organization for vehicle construction concerns
Kollektive	(collective) - team consisting of several workers
Kombinat	(combine) - group of nationalized concerns with the same production profile, including suppliers; successor of the VVB.
Neuerer	(innovators) - workers who submitted improvements for work processes

Planschuldner	(plan defaulters) - concerns that did not meet production targets.
PSR	Plan sozialistischer Realisierung (socialist realization plan) - the PSR contained instructions on intensification, modernization, labour-saving etc.
SDAG Wismut	Soviet-German Company for uranium mining
VEB	Volkseigener Betrieb (Nationalized concern) - all concerns that were expropriated or nationalized after the war or in 1972.
VVB	Vereinigung Volkseigener Betriebe (Organization of Nationalized Concerns) - successor to industrial management organs like IFA, for example
VVV	Vertrauensleutevollversammlung (plenary meeting of persons in a position of trust) - advisory committee of trade union functionaries in the collectives
SED	Sozialistische Einheitspartei Deutschlands (Socialist Unity Party of Germany - the East German Communist Party
ZBGL	Zentrale Betriebsgewerkschaftsleitung (Central concern trade union leadership)
ZMMM	Zentrale Messe der Meister von morgen (Central trade fair for tomorrow's masters) - show for young people's scientific and technical achievements
ZK	Zentralkomitee (Central Committee) - supreme organ of the SED between party conferences
ZPL	Zentrale Parteileitung (Central Party Leadership)

The Zwickau car production range

The route taken by car building in the GDR is clear from the private cars produced in Zwickau after the Second World War.

The P 240 "Sachsenring", a prestige vehicle reminiscent of Horch automobiles built before the war is completely different from the small cars that gained favour later, which had to be functional and economical above all. They illustrate clearly that in fact there was no fundamental further development after the 60s. The P 70, the first Trabant P 50, its successors the P60 and the P601 were ultimately variations on a single model. The Trabant 1.1 with its four-stroke engine certainly had improved "inner" values but its bodywork was scarcely different from the P 601.

*The P 240 "Sachsen-
ring" limousine (year
of manufacture 1954)*

The first small car
from Zwickau, the
P 70 (year of manu-
facture 1955).

The P 240 as an
estate car with
folding roof (year of
manufacture 1955).

*The Trabant P 50
with two-tone paint-
work (year of manu-
facture 1957).*

*The P 601 limousine
(year of manufac-
ture 1964).*

The P 601 Universal estate (year of manu-facture 1964).

The Trabant 1.1, here in the "Tramp" convertible version (year of manu-facture 1989).

About the author

Jürgen Schiebert was born on 7 July 1948 in Dahme in Brandenburg. He passed his school leaving examination in Brandenburg an der Havel in 1967 and at the same time trained as a concrete worker. He studied German and history at the Friedrich-Schiller-Universität in Jena from 1967 to 1971.

In 1972 he started work as an editor on the daily newspaper "Freiheit" in the Halle district, remaining in this job until 1977. From 1977 to 1978 he was employed as a concrete worker by BMK Chemie in Eisleben. He then decided on public relations work and worked in the public relations department of the Thomas-Müntzer-Theater in Eisleben from 1978 to 1980. From there he moved into the motor industry. He took over direction of public relations in the VEB Sachsenring Automobilwerke Zwickau on 1981. He also went through the stormy period after the fall of the Berlin Wall in November 1989 there.

In 1990 he was appointed Public Relations Manager of the Volkswagen-Audi-Vertriebs GmbH in Chemnitz. Jürgen Schiebert has worked in the sales promotion department of Volkswagen in the north-east region since 1992.

Planwirtschaft
auf Rädern

Wie der Trabi gebaut wurde

Planwirtschaft auf Rädern: Wie der Trabant gebaut wurde
PAL, VHS, colour, 38 mins, DEM 19.80 per copy (recommended retail price, plus DEM 6,- for postage and packing)

This video can be obtained from
MIXX – lunch, gifts, entertainment & more
Einsteinufer 63-65 · D-10587 Berlin · Tel. +49-30-34 78 62 40
Fax +49-30-34 78 62 45 · Internet: http://www.mixx.de